Product Development

Innovation Teams: Organizing for Success in New Product Development

Copyright

Reproduction

Disclaimer

Get to the Point Books
14110 Dallas Parkway, Suite 270
Dallas, Texas 75254-4379
Telephone: 972-759-0737
Fax: 972-385-7884
Email: joan.lahti@gettothepointbooks.com
Web: www.gettothepointbooks.com

Get to the Point Books

By Teresa Jurgens-Kowal, Ph.D.

Practical Project Management in a Nutshell

A Necessary Evil: The Budget

Table of Contents

Introduction

Everywhere you turn today, you see the word *innovation*: innovation in automobiles, innovation in hairstyles, innovation in electronics, and innovation in business. Ask any CEO and he or she will tell you that "innovation" is at the top of his or her priority list. But just what is innovation and how do we make it work?

Most professionals agree that innovation is defined as the commercial introduction of a new or improved technology in a product or service into a current or new market. A key word in this definition is *commercial* since innovations require the product or service to be salable. New technologies and new scientific discoveries are exciting to be sure, yet without sales of a product or service, they are simply inventions.

Innovations may lead to a new tangible product, such as a new vitamin-enhanced soda or a new laptop computer battery. Innovations also include new intangible products such as software or cloud computing databases. Innovations may also include new services such as credit card processing or on-line training webinars. In this book, we will use the convention where "product" refers to both tangible and intangible goods and services. We will also use the terms "innovation" and "new product development" interchangeably.

Chapter 1

Why is New Product Development (NPD) Different?

New Product Development (NPD) is an important way for firms to deliver value to their shareholders. Companies are in business to make money, and innovation is the only long-term activity that can deliver sustained top-line growth to firms. Companies can also grow through mergers and acquisition, but an astounding number of these ventures fail to meet their business growth objectives.

Businesses can also increase value to the shareholder through operational efficiencies. As described in our companion book, *A Necessary Evil: The Budget* (also available from Get to the Point Books), every dollar saved in business expenses contributes directly to the bottom-line profit. Yet without continued growth in sales, the factory, or manufacturing plant is limited in how much can be cut in operating expenses while still maintaining product quality. Additionally, as operating expenses are continuously scaled back, product quality begins to suffer leading to reduced sales, which in turn require even further cuts in operating expenses. Innovation is the only way out of this death spiral.

Innovation can bring new sales revenues from markets that were previously untapped, thereby boosting company profits, yet innovation does not come without some risk. Appropriately managing the uncertainty of new product development through teamwork leads to a higher degree of success and profitability.

Technology and Market Risk

In fact, all new product development comes with some degree of risk. We'll talk about different types of NPD projects in a later chapter but for now let's assume a radical innovation involves both a new technology and a new market while an incremental innovation includes technology improvements for a product in an existing market. It's fairly easy to imagine that a radical innovation may involve substantial risk to the business – the technology may not work as originally envisioned or the market share may not materialize. Financial outcomes, calculated by return on investment (ROI) and net present value (NPV), are often discounted by risk factors called "the probability of technical success" and "the probability of commercial success" to account for the uncertainty of introducing a radical innovation.

Incremental innovations, on the other hand, also involve a degree of risk. While the improved technical objectives are quite likely to be met with success, customers may not be willing to pay a higher price for the new product. Equally uncertain is the prospect of a competitor introducing a higher quality product with more features at a lower price or a new technology that makes your product obsolete.

Consider, for example, that cell phones have made personal digital assistants (PDAs) nearly obsolete. Conversely, incremental innovations can lead to feature-heavy products that are expensive to manufacture yet add little value for the end-user.

These technology and market risks make innovating new products distinct from all other business processes. Operational improvements can squeeze out a few more units per hour on the assembly line to reduce costs and cheaper parts can replace ones that are more expensive; we can predict the outcome of these changes with a high degree of certainty. However, introduction of a radically new technology in the marketplace may be greeted with a run on store shelves or a collective yawn from consumers. Since the long-term viability of a firm is staked on innovating new products, we must learn how to innovate and how to do it well.

Teams in the Workplace

At the same time, CEOs have recognized that innovation is the only way to sustain long-term profitability enhancement and organizations have recognized that teams are the most capable structure to accomplish work. Employee teams have a variety of positive benefits.

- Increased responsibility.
- Improved accountability.
- Optimized use of resources.
- Higher performance.
- Increased job satisfaction.

We define a team as a group of people with complementary skills that are committed to a common purpose and to which they hold themselves mutually accountable. Complementary skills are especially important for new product development, but we'll discuss more about that later.

Teams can take many forms. For example, permanent teams may be organized around a specific work function and remain intact as long as the firm is in business. Individual team members may come and go, yet the permanent team's purpose remains constant over a very long period of time. Consider the information technology (IT) department at a firm. The team is tasked with the mission of maintaining the computer systems of the company. Because the company expects to be doing business for many years into the future, the IT team is permanent. Whereas one team member may be assigned to perform maintenance on laptops this month, a different computer specialist may help out next month since the other team member has been reassigned to other tasks.

In contrast, a temporary team is one with a well-defined mission and has a specific starting point and ending point (when the project objectives are complete). Temporary teams may be organized for a few days, a few weeks, or a few years for the most complex projects.

Teams may be composed of a set of work group experts, such as the engineering team or the sales team, or the team can be comprised of cross-functional representatives. We will be discussing more about the specific structure of cross-functional NPD teams in Chapter 3.

The bookkeeping staff at your firm prepares the monthly financial reports and assists with special requests for data. Would you consider this team a permanent or temporary team? Why?

Answers are in Appendix 1.

Other descriptions of teams focus on the management and leadership of the task force. A directed work group often takes instruction from a department manager, while an empowered and autonomous team may be self-directed. In the latter case, team members assign tasks to themselves as well as take on supervisory and administrative roles.

Finally, teams may be physically co-located or they may be "virtual" teams, dispersed by geography and conducting their work primarily via electronic means. As computing power soars and businesses become more globally competitive, virtual teams are becoming the norm rather than the exception. In fact, virtual teams are so important to accomplishing innovation goals that we've dedicated an entire chapter to tips and hints for high performing virtual teams (see Chapter 6).

There are also a number of specific types of teams used in new product development, which we will describe in detail in Chapter 3. These specific teams are often suited to particular types of innovation projects. So let's turn first to some common definitions and examples of NPD project types.

Chapter 2

Types of NPD Projects

In the previous chapter, we began describing the various ranges of risk and uncertainty involved with new product development. Innovation necessarily encompasses a *technology risk*—can we find the right technical solution to a problem?—and *market risk*—can we sell the product or service for a satisfactory profit? If we plot these two ranges of uncertainty against one another, as in Figure 1, we can identify and name the four quadrants of risk or four common innovation project types.

Figure 1

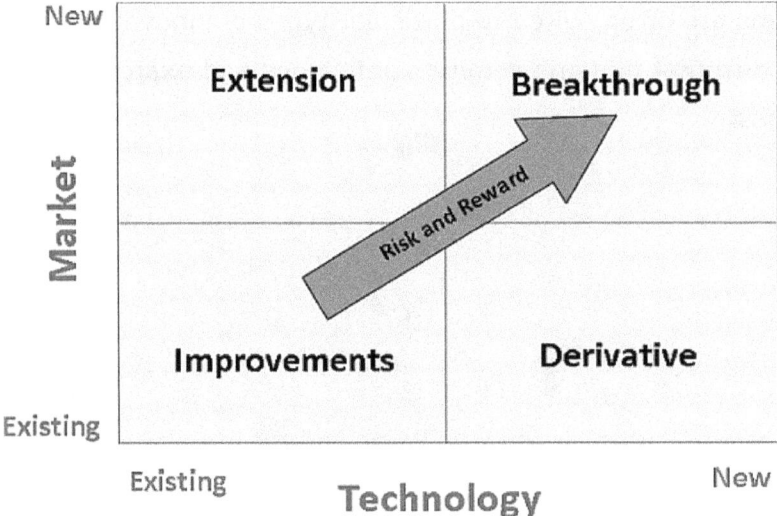

Breakthrough Projects

As shown in Figure 1, breakthrough innovation projects involve both high technology risk and high market uncertainty. Normally, a breakthrough project will include significant research and development (R&D) efforts in a new technical arena. R&D for breakthrough projects may take a substantial effort in both human resources and financial investment. An example of a breakthrough project is e-ink, which created the ability for handheld e-Readers to display text with little power consumption. This breakthrough technical development allows e-Readers, smartphones, and tablet computers to display text quickly without significantly draining the device's battery.

Breakthrough technical developments yield products that change how consumers interact with their environment. In conjunction, a breakthrough market development, also a high-risk endeavor, involves identifying a set of customers that will repeatedly purchase and use the radically new technology.

As with the breakthrough technical development, identifying a specific target market that is willing to try a brand new product can cost a company much in time, human resource effort, and expenses to develop the market. Often the first consumers to accept a new technology are in a fringe market. These customers like to try new technologies and value being the **first** to own a new product.

Of course, the company is at significant financial risk if they miss the target of the initial market acceptance or penetration rate. Generally, new product acceptance in the marketplace is assumed to follow a normal distribution, as shown in Figure 2, where the x-axis represents time after commercialization.

Figure 2

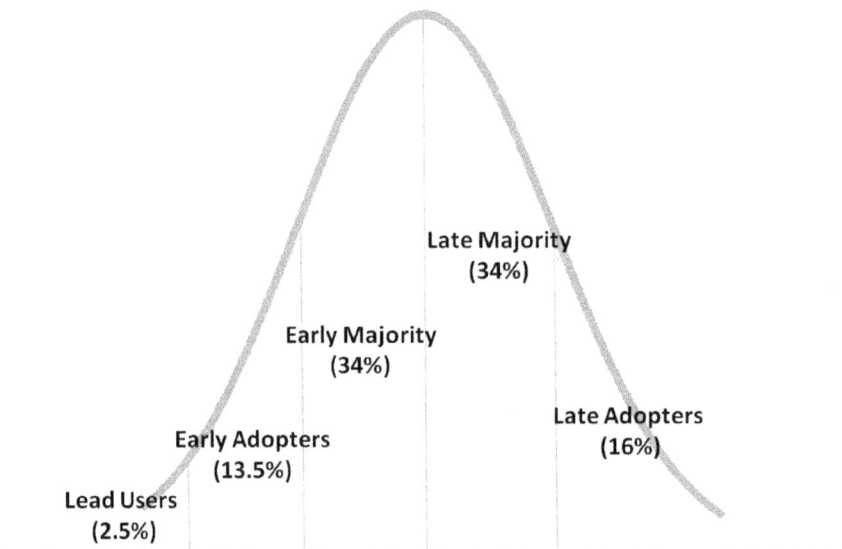

Market penetration requires that lead users, or the fringe customers, accept the new product and begin using it shortly after commercial launch. These lead users make up a very small percentage of the market—about 2.5%. As the early adopters and early majority, the next 13.5% and 34% of the market, begin to try, purchase, and use the new product, the firm begins realizing profits on their breakthrough innovation.

Breakthrough innovations mandate a strong, cohesive NPD team made up of representatives from R&D, manufacturing, and marketing. We will discuss the ideal type of innovation team for developing breakthrough new products in a later chapter.

Test Your Knowledge

Suppose your firm manufactures pencils. A member of your sales team comes to you and indicates that he has learned of a large demand for colored pencils that have red points on one end and green points on the other end. What type of NPD project is this and why?

Answers are in Appendix 1.

Platform Projects

A special type of breakthrough innovation is the platform project. Platform products have a common architecture or technology basis that is utilized across a wide variety of products called a product family. Like a breakthrough product, a platform product may require months and years of technical research and market development. Furthermore, like a breakthrough product, platform projects may involve higher technology risk and market uncertainty. If the company is banking on successful development of a new technical component, that is core to the new product family, significant losses can occur if the technology cannot be made to work. Often, new product releases of derivative products are planned over a multi-year period, with the platform technology at the heart of the product family (see the discussion later in this chapter).

For example, assume a company manufactures motorized garden equipment such as lawnmowers, weed trimmers, and chainsaws. The common core architecture for these devices is a small yet powerful gasoline engine; the engine is the platform for the product family. Because future product releases include automatic transmission lawnmowers, double-string weed trimmers, and 12-inch chainsaws, successful engine development is crucial to the success of the product platform.

While a firm will realize the highest long-term profit from platform products introduced to new markets, platform technologies are also successful in existing markets as long as the firm can quickly establish consequential market share for the platform products.

Examples of platform products abound: chocolate sandwich cookies with a double or triple layer of icing, mint flavoring of the cookie or icing, colored icing for the holiday cookies, and chocolate-dipped sandwich cookies. Each of these varieties is considered either a product extension or derivative, which we will address next.

Extensions

Product extension projects are represented in the upper-left quadrant of Figure 1. Here, the product is using a known technology in a new market. Sometimes, these are called "repositioning" projects because the primary work activity for the NPD team is to place the product into a new market. Little traditional R&D activity is conducted in order to launch an extension product. Thus, the technical program is at the lower end of the risk spectrum.

As shown earlier in Figure 2, lead users and early adopters in the new market must be willing to try the product and to purchase it in the new application environment. The product should be thoroughly field tested in the new application to ensure customers in the new target market want and need the innovation.

A classic example of a product extension is the sport-utility vehicle (SUV). Many of the early models of SUVs utilized the same engine, transmission, and chassis as a standard sedan. However, the SUVs were marketed to an underserved customer base that needed more vehicle storage space than a car offered. The technology for these early model SUVs was only slightly modified from a sedan, yet the market initially required significant development effort and long-term success was uncertain.

Other NPD extensions fit within the special category of platform projects as described above. Suppose the firm that manufactures yard equipment wishes to extend the small engine platform to a new market. A logical extension is to sell hedge trimmers. The technical development for a hedge trimmer is at low risk for failure since the firm already can manufacture the small gasoline engine and has the capability to produce other cutting and trimming devices, such as chainsaws and wee trimmers, respectively. Yet the hedge trimmer is sold into a commercial market rather than the do-it-yourself garden market like the lawn mower and weed trimmer. Significant development thus is required to ensure customers recognize the separate market for hedge trimmers. With pruning shears as the only competition in the marketplace, the firm can likely overcome any market uncertainties for the successful innovation of a small gasoline-powered hedge trimmer.

Derivative Projects

In the lower right-hand quadrant of Figure 1, we note the derivative project. Derivative innovations are products that utilize new technologies and that are sold into existing markets. This is one of the most common types of projects in new product development.

Derivatives may range in complexity from simple additions of new or improved product features to substantially different technical capabilities offering a new interface for the customer. What is unique to the derivative product compared to breakthroughs and extensions is that the market is already well established. Most new or improved products fall into this category, which requires significant R&D work yet little market uncertainty for the commercial products. An example of a simple derivative product is that of smartphone applications (or "apps"). Previous releases of smartphones allowed users to download apps to access social media and other websites like Facebook, Twitter, or the weather. A derivative innovation for the smartphone comes with these apps pre-loaded on the device and available on the phone's home touch screen.

A more complex derivative project in new product development may involve the addition of features to an existing product. Oftentimes these features are requested by the customers currently using the product like the easy access smartphone apps or other more complex features. For illustrative purposes, consider the feature addition of a GPS to many vehicle dashboards. In the base case, the technology of the car (engine, transmission, and chassis) is unchanged as is the market, yet adding a GPS requires a large amount of R&D to ensure adequate power supply, effective antenna, placement for a user-friendly interface, and a number of safety interlocks to prevent the GPS from being tampered with by a driver when the car is in motion. These technical developments are costly for the firm in terms of R&D expenditures and human resources. Furthermore, the risk of technical failure is high since the GPS is primarily an electronics system and not core to the manufacturing or assembly of the vehicle.

Finally, derivatives are frequently modeled for innovation in the special class of platform projects discussed above. Platform architectures are designed with the fundamental concept that features and attributes will be added to or enhanced over the initial platform product rollout. Earlier we described chocolate sandwich cookies as a platform product. Derivative products include the double icing sandwich cookies, holiday-colored icing sandwich cookies, and chocolate dipped sandwich cookies. Conversely, extension products would include a frozen ice cream cookie sandwich, which would be sold through different markets. In the next chapters, we will discuss NPD project team structures that are best suited for derivative and platform projects.

Test Your Knowledge

Your company manufactures pet food. One very popular product line is tuna for cats. You currently sell tuna in cans and are considering selling a tuna/salmon blend as well. You are also considering selling a tuna/whitefish blend in cans and a flaked tuna product available in snack-sized portions. Describe these innovation projects.

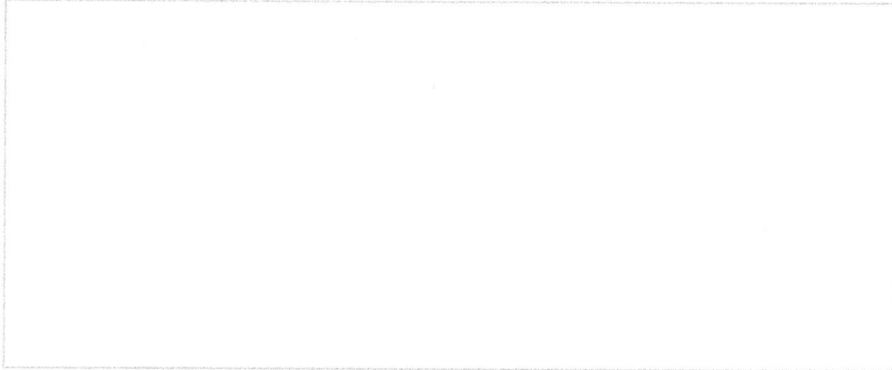

Answers are in Appendix 1.

Improvement Projects

In the lower left quadrant of Figure 1, new products that include development in existing markets with existing technologies are referred to as *improvements*. Generally, these are low risk projects from both a technological and market perspective. However, the full life cycle return on investment (ROI) for improvement projects also tends to be less substantial than for projects with more novelty.

Many improvement projects involve reducing costs, especially in the manufacturing process. Some sources do not consider manufacturing modifications as innovation work; however, it is prudent to consider any project as new product development if there is any potential impact to the end-user or consumer.

A predominant form of cost reduction project seeks to supply lower cost parts and raw materials in an existing product. Of course, limited

R&D studies should be conducted to ensure the product continues to meet all quality standards that the marketplace anticipates. In the chemical, food and beverage, and pharmaceutical industries, alternative raw material suppliers must be certified that the compounds meet required purity standards, and the R&D and quality departments must validate quality and confirm that unknown reactions do not occur.

Other process improvement projects may include different equipment in the factory or even outsourcing portions of the manufacturing process to achieve improved financial measures. Again, these products improvements should be transparent to the customer and are therefore low risk in a market perspective. In addition, the technical effort is also limited and of low uncertainty for new product development success. Simple product improvements that are transparent to the end-user should offer value with little or no cost.

Finally, another unfortunate category of product improvement involves correcting errors or faults with an existing product. These types of projects are the least rewarding financially since they only preserve sales, but they are required to save a brand in the case of poor performing products that were already launched. Of course, the market risk is relatively low since the company **must** fix the problem to maintain presence in the market. Technical risks are also low since troubleshooting and repairing the dysfunctional part or mechanism is expected. Automotive recalls are an example of a product improvement with no profit margin, low market risk, and low technical uncertainty.

Review

Let's quickly review the four types of innovation projects shown in Figure 1. Breakthrough projects have high technical risk and high market uncertainty. Product extensions involve repositioning an existing product into a new market so these projects have a low technical risk coupled with a high market risk. Derivative products, which may build upon a special type of breakthrough project called the platform product, typically have substantial technical risk yet moderately low market risk. Finally, projects that introduce slightly modified or improved features to the market or are designed for cost savings are called improvement projects. Moving from the lower left to the upper right in Figure 1 will both increase the risk and reward involved in the new product development effort.

In the next chapter, we will describe the characteristics of four standard innovation teams then we will match these project types with team types in Chapter 4.

Chapter 3

Structure of NPD Teams

New product development teams come in many shapes and sizes, depending on factors such as

- Complexity of the project.
- Time line for completion (introduction to the market).
- Newness of the technology.
- Requirements of customers and the market.
- Culture of the organization.

Recall that a team is defined as a small group of people with complementary skills who have a common purpose and to which they hold themselves mutually accountable.

For innovation projects, we recommend that the core group of team members number six to ten. Simple NPD projects, such as improvements and some derivatives or extension projects may not require any additional team members to complete the work; however, projects that are more complex will utilize sub-teams and auxiliary team members for successful product introduction. Holding the core team to a small group of people allows for more efficient decision-making and helps maintain clear lines of responsibility for each functional representative. Some teams insist upon an odd number of members so that democratic voting can be used in the decision-making process, while others rely on the team leader or upper management to clarify any impasse the team might face.

Cross-Functional Teams

One of the most important considerations for any new product development team is cross-functional representation. Cross-functional teams require members from each department that will be impacted by the new innovation. Figure 3 illustrates a few of the departments that may be represented on an NPD team.

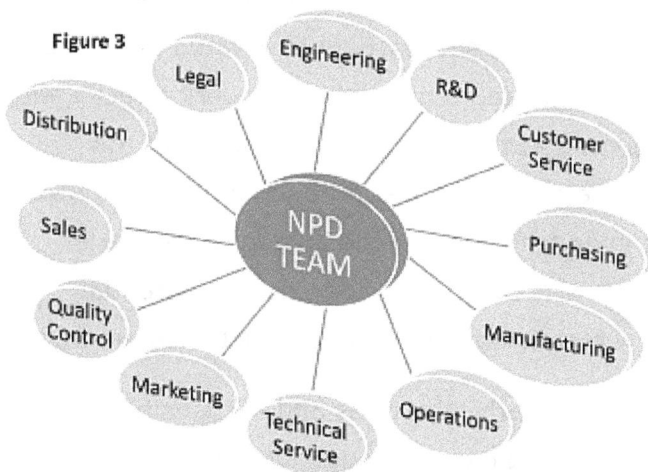

Figure 3

Of course, not every department shown in Figure 3 will send a representative to serve as a core team member. Even so, each department should be informed regarding the innovation effort so each can plan and prepare for the new product launch. Various departments will have more or less involvement at different stages of the NPD project as well.

For instance, the legal department may play a role early in the idea generation stages of new product development to ensure that the innovation being pursued is not already protected by competitor patents. As the new technology is researched and built into a commercially viable product, the legal department will assume a stronger role to ensure the new technology is protected by intellectual property (patents, trademarks, and so forth).

On the other hand, the R&D team members will have a substantial role throughout all stages of the new product development effort. First, they play a key role in investigating and designing the new technology. Second, R&D will interface extensively with marketing to ensure customers' needs and wants are successfully translated into product specifications. Next, the R&D team members will work directly with the factory operations group to ensure proper scale-up of the technology from lab-scale to commercial production. Finally, R&D group members may even transfer into the customer service or technical service department in order to address any potential problems with the new technology after the product is commercialized.

R	Responsible
A	Accountable
C	Consult
I	Inform

Clearly, the roles and responsibilities of the core cross-functional team members can vary significantly. One tool that can help an NPD team and manages communications within the core team and with the extended team members (e.g. legal) is the RACI chart. RACI stands for Responsible, Accountable, Consult, and Inform.

You can learn more about using a RACI chart in our companion eBook, *Practical Project Management in a Nutshell*, also available from Get to the Point Books.

Test Your Knowledge

Suppose you have a team composed of Larry, an electrical engineer; Mary Kay, an electronics specialist; and Lee, a journeyman electrician. The team is tasked with adding a circuit breaker to the factory. Is this a cross-functional team?

Answers are in Appendix 1.

Functional Work Groups

In this book, we follow the team definitions attributed to Wheelwright and Clark (Wheelwright & Clark, 1992).

- Functional Work Groups.
- Lean Teams.
- Full Teams.
- Venture Teams.

We'll describe each of these types of NPD teams in turn, and, in the next chapter, we'll match up the recommended team structure with the types of innovation projects previously discussed in Chapter 2.

A functional work group is a very weak team structure for innovation. The functional work group generally is **not** composed of cross-functional team members, and it should only be utilized for the simplest of NPD projects. An illustration of the workflow for a functional work group is shown in Figure 4 on the following page.

Notice in Figure 4 that a functional work group team member is shown by the image in the circle. Because the work group representative is still contained within the rectangle (illustrating the functional department), the team member's task assignments are directed by the functional department manager. Also, note that an idea progresses to commercialization in an ad-hoc manner, moving from department to department sequentially.

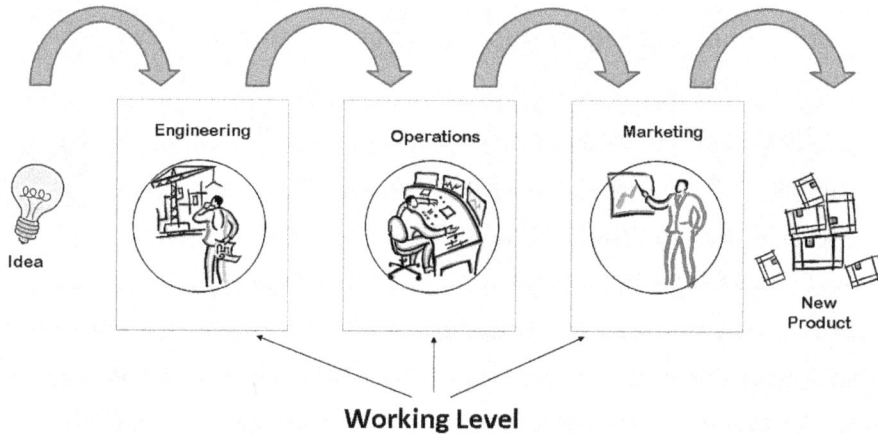

Figure 4

Idea → Engineering → Operations → Marketing → New Product

Working Level

Functional work groups, in fact, have very little cross-functional representation, and innovation projects may be slow to progress to commercialization for this reason. The arrows shown above the rectangles in Figure 4 indicate that the new product development effort moves from department to department in a linear fashion, not concurrently as would occur in a high performing, cross-functional team.

Other characteristics of a functional work group follow.

- Typically, no named or appointed team leader.
- Non-influential project manager (if a project manager is named at all).
- Tasks progress in an ad-hoc manner.
- Team members' allegiance is to the department.
- Weak and uncoordinated communication.
- Innovation work is conducted in "silos."

Functional work groups are highly dependent on existing inter-departmental relationships to get innovation work accomplished. Consider that Bart used to work in operations and he is now assigned to the R&D group. Bart's idea for a new product will require a few changes in the production equipment, so he calls Marjorie in operations to discuss the idea. Meanwhile, Lana is new to the company yet she had previously worked for a competitor. Lana knows that her idea for an improved technology will be met with a strong and encouraging market response. Even so, Lana has not been with the company long enough to have established relationships with marketing or operations to implement her new idea under a predominant functional work group structure.

Undoubtedly, the functional work group structure can sometimes be frustrating to the individuals working on an innovation effort. The team members' task assignments and performance are measured against *department* goals and not those of the NPD project. As we'll discuss in the next chapter, functional work group teams are inappropriate except for the simplest of NPD project types.

Lean Teams

The structure of a lean team is shown in Figure 5. As with the functional work group structure, team members continue to report directly to a functional department manager. However, as indicated by the arrow that shows work progress across **all** represented departments, the lean team employs a weak cross-functional organizational structure implemented through the role of a part-time project leader.

Liaisons from each department are named to interact with the project manager. For these relatively simple NPD projects, the project manager and team members may be assigned only part-time, and it may be the project manager's very first supervisory role.

Figure 5

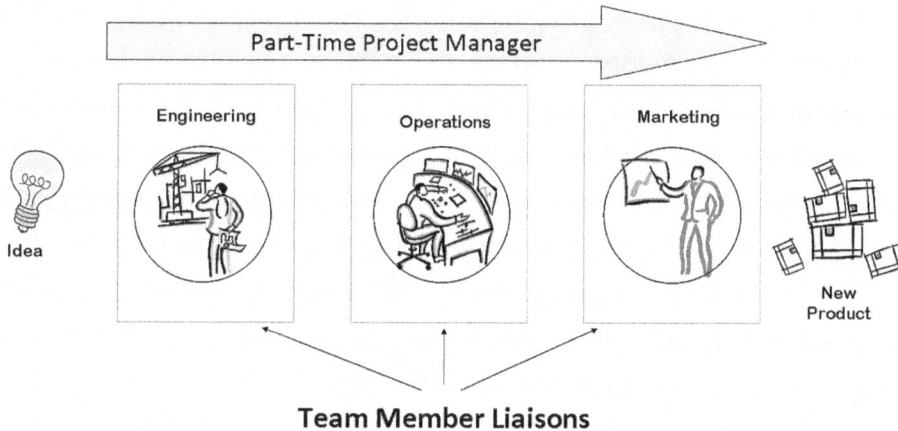

Team Member Liaisons

Compared to the functional work group, a lean team has improved coordination and communication. The NPD project likely has a written charter with specific goals and objectives so that the team leader or project manager can ensure on-time delivery of the new commercial product.

Unfortunately, the lean team structure may still prove frustrating to some individuals. Team member liaisons continue to report to the functional department managers whose performance goals may be at odds with the innovation project. However, because at least a part-time project team leader has been assigned to ensure a quality product launch, the functional department managers are aware of the project's needs. The RACI chart described on page 22 and more fully in *Practical Project Management in a Nutshell*, is particularly useful to communicate roles and responsibilities for the lean team.

Full Teams

Figure 6, illustrating a full innovation team, is not radically different from the lean team as represented in Figure 5. Note that the project manager has a stronger role than in the lean team, in that he or she reports to the executive team. Additionally, the full team members are now called out by name and specific contribution as team members. In fact, the core team members of the full team may also be team leaders of auxiliary teams necessary to complete the moderately complex new product development project.

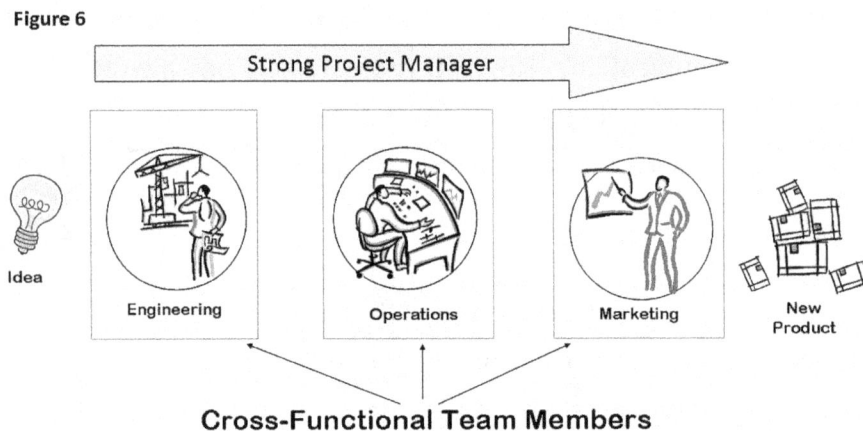

Figure 6

Strong Project Manager

Idea

Engineering

Operations

Marketing

New Product

Cross-Functional Team Members

Within a full team, work coordination is highly aligned and structured. Team meetings will be held on a routine basis, and management systems are formally established such as shared databases, work procedures and policies, design standards, and information technology tracking. Team communications, both within the NPD effort and external to the team, are frequent and well managed by an experienced team leader.

The team leader for a full team is a full-time project manager as are the core team members. Core team members continue to report to a functional department manager (as indicated by the circles enclosed within the rectangles in Figure 6). However, senior management fully expects that department managers will support the innovation effort, so that NPD team members' task assignments and performance reviews include a majority contribution to the project. The project manager's performance appraisal of NPD team members is thus very important, yet the department manager retains responsibility for the individual's career progression.

While individual team members are generally more satisfied with the innovation challenges of working full-time on a full team, some functional experts may be overcommitted. If the firm is working on several NPD projects simultaneously, these subject matter experts can potentially bottleneck the innovation efforts.

Suppose that Nathaniel is the subject matter expert in the childcare market at a firm that manufactures bedding. New Product Development projects are underway for non-flammable sheets, thin but warm blankets of a new fabric, and a cartoon-inspired duvet and pillowcase set. Nathaniel's expertise on the consumer tastes and market share is required for each project, even though Sam, Peggy, and Evan are assigned, respectively, as full team members on each specific project. Moreover, with good project planning, Nathaniel's role in each NPD project can be managed so that each product is launched on time.

Thus, the characteristics of a full team are
- Well-coordinated project tasks.
- Extensive and frequent communications.
- Cross-functional representation.
- Project management tools used to plan and execute work tasks.
- Performance metrics aligned with the project goals.

Test Your Knowledge

Is it possible to use a full team for a new product development project that is also a new platform?

Answers are in Appendix 1.

Venture Teams

A venture team is used for the most complex and challenging types of new product development, as we will describe in more detail in Chapter 4. As implied in the name, a venture team is often a standalone innovation effort in a joint venture or spin-off business line for the corporation. Venture teams should be physically co-located at a different site than the mainstream business and are operated by a very experienced senior executive as the project leader. Venture teams will have their own budget to develop and commercialize the new product. Figure 7 illustrates the structure of a venture team.

Figure 7

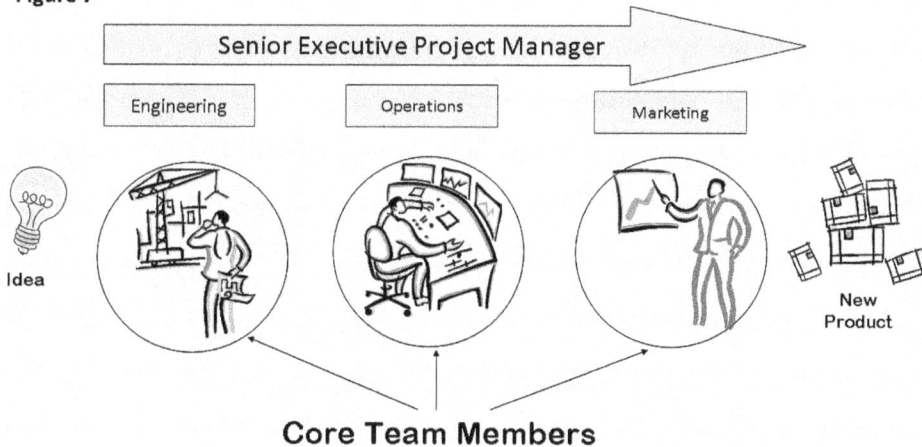

In Figure 7, the core team members, illustrated by circles for the firm's three functions, are placed *outside of* and *separate from* the functional departments (represented by the rectangles). This is because the core venture team members are assigned full time to the innovation project and now report directly to the project manager rather than a functional department manager. Thus, team members' task assignments are directed **solely** by the venture team leader.

Of course, by definition, the venture team is comprised of cross-functional members. Products launched by a venture team often become spin-off businesses or separate business lines; therefore, all functions necessary to operate, as a standalone business should be represented in the innovation effort.

Venture teams often have little communication with the base business. As we'll see in the next chapter, venture teams are frequently employed to develop radically new technologies for unique target customers. Consequently, it is sometimes beneficial to sequester the NPD venture team in a separate location.

A classic example of a venture team is the one used by IBM in the 1970s and 1980s to design and develop a commercial personal computer (PC). IBM's expertise was in the mainframe computer technology yet the marketplace was demanding PCs. IBM chartered a venture team in Boca Raton, Florida, with very little connection to the mother corporation for the project.

Coordination of work and communications between team members is very high. Since all of the core team members and sub-team members report to the same project manager, the work effort is tightly aligned to accomplish the innovation project's specific goals and objectives.

One of the most significant challenges to a venture team is placing team members back into their home organizations **after** the completion of the project. Opportunities to work on venture teams typically arise only a couple of times through most people's careers. It is exciting to work on highly stimulating and challenging innovation projects that are new-to-the-world. Some individuals find returning to slower-paced, day-to-day routine work is a letdown after a venture team's rapid-fire challenges. This is another reason why many products are spun-off or held in separate business units after the new technology is commercialized in the new market. Table 1 summarizes the characteristics of the four types of NPD teams.

Table 1

TEAM CHARACTERISTIC	FUNCTIONAL WORK GROUP	LEAN TEAM	FULL TEAM	VENTURE TEAM
Cross-Functional	No	Yes	Strong	Strong
Coordination of Work	Ad Hoc	Some	Yes	Strong
Internal Communication	Weak	Yes	Strong	Strong
External Communication	Not Typical	Yes	Yes	Maybe
Performance Appraisals	Department	Department	Department	Project
Team Leader	NO	Weak	Strong	Senior Executive
Biggest Challenge	Time Delivery	Department vs. Project	Use of Experts	Re-Integrate to Home Organization

Chapter 4

Matching Innovation Project and Team Types

New Product Development is a unique business activity. It is the number one way to grow profitably a business but is technically risky with uncertain markets. The level of risk varies with the type of innovation project. Odds of success in NPD can be improved by properly staffing projects with a team structure that is best matched to the risk and complexity of work. Table 2 summarizes this matchup, which we'll discuss next.

Table 2

Innovation Team Type	NPD Project Type			
	Breakthrough	Extension	Derivative	Improvement
Functional Work Group		*Situational*	*Situational*	**Recommended**
Lean Team		**Recommended**	**Recommended**	*Situational*
Full Team	*Situational*	**Recommended**	**Recommended**	
Venture Team	**Recommended**			

Darkly shaded cells in Table 2 represent the recommended NPD team structure for each project type while lightly shaded cells are acceptable team structures provided that other conditions can be met within the organization.

For example, in Chapter 2 we indicated that improvement projects often include cost reduction initiatives such as raw material substitutions or outsourcing the parts inventory. These types of projects - that have low technical risk (existing technology) and very low market uncertainty (existing customers) - can be developed by a functional work group.

Changes to the product through a raw material substitution, for instance, should be transparent to the customer. As long as the purchasing department and quality control personnel can validate and certify the less expensive raw materials and the final product quality, we would expect the work could be conducted with little or no coordination and communication with other functions. The effort can be spearheaded by an ambitious employee who does not require a team to accomplish the simple objectives of cutting expenses. Project goals are aligned with the department deliverables and the functional department manager can adequately assess the individual's performance on a straightforward improvement project.

Projects that are new in only one dimension, technology or market, are best executed by either a lean team or a full team, as indicated in

Table 2. Consider a product family extension in which the firm is adding a lemon-basil gardener scrub to its line of handmade soaps. In this case, the target market is new yet not substantially different from existing markets. Thus, a cross-functional team is required to ensure the small technical development is timed to meet the new market introduction. The part-time project manager is in her first supervisory assignment after working in the marketing department for nearly five years. She is able to coordinate activities and tasks with permission from the various department managers and the product is launched on time and quite successfully.

A project with more complexity, such as, a platform derivative product, which includes doubling the battery life of an electronic, handheld gaming device while also adding customer-requested features, may be executed with a full team. In this case, the cross-functional team members must have frequent communication regarding design changes and decisions to ensure the product can be manufactured and sold commercially within a given time period because competitors are also working on longer battery life. The project will require a strong and experienced team leader and will likely have its own budget. Additional sub-teams and non-core team members necessitate formal communication to apply for technology patents and to train the customer service organization on the new features. The full team may be in place for several months in order to successfully design and launch this new derivative product.

Occasionally, a full team can capture breakthrough products. However, the organization must be willing to allow full team members latitude to work on the NPD project without conflicting department goals. Additionally, the project team should be co-located on a separate floor of the building, at a minimum, to eliminate day-to-day functional distractions. Formal communications and organizational structures may benefit a full team working on a breakthrough or platform project.

Even so, significant breakthrough innovations should be executed by a venture team in most circumstances. A firm is staking future growth on the breakthrough or platform development and proper resourcing of the project can lead to higher odds of success. Breakthrough product development efforts involve simultaneous new technical development with new market growth; therefore, these projects are best handled by a highly integrated cross-functional team. Intra-team communication and task coordination is at the highest possible level while external communications from the team to potential customers, ad agencies, and the legal department are coordinated by the team leader. Project managers of venture teams are highly experienced individuals from the senior management ranks. He or she is responsible for a large product development budget and performance appraisals for each team member.

Venture teams will be comprised of several sub-teams in order to accomplish the innovation work efficiently. For example, to develop a solar-powered bicycle engine, the breakthrough innovation will require sub-teams to develop the engine, the transmission, and solar batteries, as well as the marketing and sales staff, purchasing and distribution, and factory assembly. While each sub-team has its own team leader, all of the sub-teams work on tasks and milestones that are consolidated at the project manager level.

Test Your Knowledge

Suppose the company already has extensive expertise in solar-powered engines and markets the solar-powered engines on children's toys, like wagons and radio-controlled cars. What type of project and what type of innovation team would you recommend now?

Answers are in Appendix 1.

In this chapter, we've matched the innovation project types of Chapter 2 with the best type of NPD team from Chapter 3 to execute the project. In the remaining chapters, we'll give some brief tips on leading teams and how to manage a virtual, or dispersed team.

Chapter 5

Leadership and Team Membership

Innovation teams involve a highly diverse staff and may require new product development tasks that range from simple cost improvement projects to groundbreaking new technologies. Success of NPD teams depends on many factors.

- Common goals and purpose.
- Organization culture.
- Team relationships.
- Effective leadership.

Common Goals

Common goals and purpose should be understood by each team member and are fundamental to calling a team to action in the first instance. In fact, our definition of "team" requires that the team members rally around a common mission to launch a new product successfully.

For all except the simplest of NPD projects, we recommend documenting the project goals and objectives in a charter, often called the *Product Innovation Charter (PIC)*. A key role of the charter is to gain agreement on the innovation project deliverables and to assure senior management that the new product is aligned with the firm's mission and values. PIC documents should include the following sections:

- **Background** – why is this opportunity attractive to the firm?
- **Arenas** – which technologies and markets are addressed by this innovation project?
- **Metrics** – what measures will be utilized to determine the product and team's success?
- **Special guidelines** – are there any special regulations or considerations for this product development effort?

Generally, NPD teams should help to write the PIC and many companies encourage team members to sign the charter document. Adding one's signature to a document increases the individual's commitment to the project. It is also important for the team members to assist in determining the success metrics for the innovation project. The team leader should ensure that project objectives include stretch goals in order to challenge the team to higher levels of performance. Workers tend to perform most effectively when they are striving to meet difficult goals to which they are publicly committed. Setting goals proves to be motivational for team members as well.

Organizational Culture

Organizational culture, on the other hand, is mostly intangible and can vary between firms and even within divisions of a single corporation. Successful organization cultures for innovation allow autonomy of teams and encourage fast failure of ideas in order to generate the most valuable new products in the shortest time possible. Figure 8 on the following page, illustrates some other cultural characteristics of successful innovation teams.

Organizational culture is a set of values, beliefs, and expectations shared by the people in the organization. As indicated above, organizations have a stable existence apart from the individuals that make them up. Organizational culture consists of unwritten rules that dictate the behaviors of employees and team members. These norms include social behaviors (arriving to work on time), communication styles (written or verbal), influence and status, and informal individual and group performance rewards.

Team member relationships are dependent upon many of the characteristics delineated in Figure 8. Trust tends to top the list of intra-team behaviors when individuals are asked to describe successful teams. Project leaders set the tone for the cross-functional team relationships in how they manage meetings, communications, and task assignments.

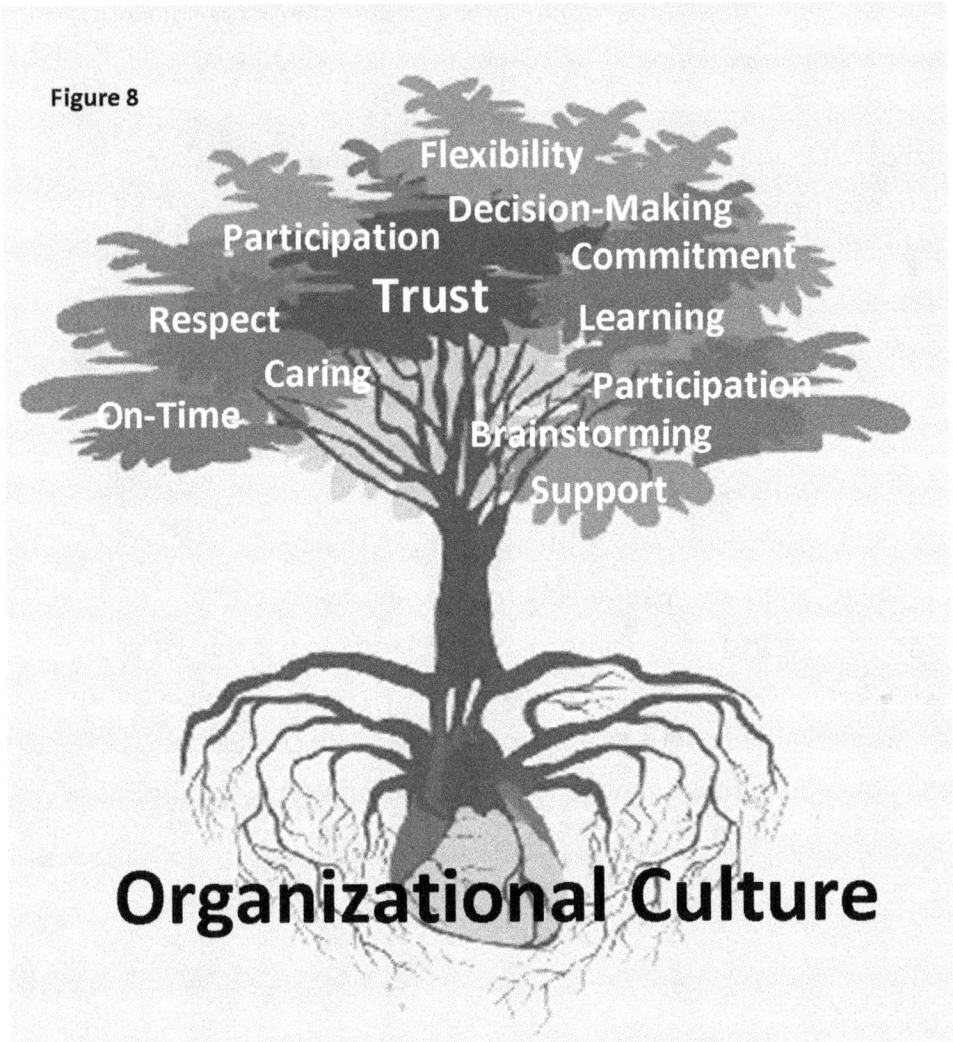

Figure 8

Flexibility
Decision-Making
Participation
Commitment
Trust
Respect
Learning
Caring
Participation
On-Time
Brainstorming
Support

Organizational Culture

Team members who are empowered to make decisions and act autonomously on behalf of the team generally demonstrate higher levels of job satisfaction and creativity in problem solving. Satisfied employees lead to more efficient product development and, therefore, more satisfied customers.

Effective leadership involves selecting individuals to work on the innovation teams, preparing an open and encouraging workspace, sharing project information broadly, cheering successes, learning from failures, and providing appropriate performance awards.

Much more can be said about effective team leadership, organizational culture, and team relationships; however, we encourage you to investigate your company's leadership development program and to experiment with different leadership styles as you begin managing a variety of innovation projects.

Chapter 6

Tips for Virtual Teams

Virtual, or dispersed, teams are fast becoming the norm. Project team experts span the globe and computers connect team members 24/7. Still, dispersed teams have many pitfalls. Geographically dispersed teams must rely on electronic communications, many of which are asynchronous and certainly lack the emotional and subtle clues given by body language in typical face-to-face communication. Team members from different ethnic backgrounds communicate differently and use a variety of norms and standards that might not be understood or accepted on another continent.

Simple innovations, such as a cost reduction project executed by a functional work group, can often be successfully executed by a highly dispersed team. Extra time should be allowed for the product to reach commercialization in order to accommodate the high level of asynchronous communications and to facilitate the common purpose among the dispersed team members.

NPD projects with any degree of complexity in technology or market development for example lean or full teams, will need to have at least one face-to-face meeting to allow team members to build trust and relationships as discussed in the previous chapter. Projects with lower levels of technology or market development may use video or phone conferencing to establish initial contacts and to build team commitment.

However, as described in Chapter 3, full and venture teams are most successful when they are co-located. In most cases, virtual teams are not adequate to complete large-scale breakthroughs.

Some additional tips for virtual teams follow.

1. Hold an initial face-to-face meeting.

2. Ensure adequate training is conducted on all information sharing software or tools.

3. Establish a protocol for all teleconferences to ensure each team member participates.

4. Enforce team rules for timely e-mail and voicemail responses.

5. Develop a "wiki" page for all intra-team communications.

6. Empower team members to communicate on behalf of the team to their local organizations.

7. Recognize and reward team members for team behaviors.

Summary

Wrapping Up

New Product Development is a highly profitable activity in most firms, yet there are risks and uncertainties to find new technologies and to grow new markets. Innovation projects generally fall into one of four broad categories, depending on the technical risk and market uncertainty.

- Product Improvement.
- Derivative.
- Line Extension.
- Breakthrough.

A special category of products called platform products are expected to deliver profits over the long run by using a breakthrough technology as a basis for introducing derivative and extension products.

These NPD projects are best executed by innovation teams of one of the following structures.

- Functional work group.
- Lean team.
- Full team.
- Venture team.

Successful innovation teams are autonomous and empowered with effective leadership. Virtual or dispersed teams face special challenges that can be overcome by judicious attention to communications and organizational culture.

New Product Development offers a rewarding career to those who choose this field. Our hope is that by learning more about the different types of projects and innovation teams, you will be able to successfully convert creative ideas into profitable products.

Innovation is the number one way businesses can grow. Yet new product development (NPD) is fraught with technical risk and market uncertainties. In this Introduction to Innovation Teams, we described the four most common types of NPD projects based upon risk and uncertainty. Then we introduce typical innovation team structures and matched the team structure with the project type that leads to the most successful project execution.

Of course, successful teams depend upon culture and leadership. Unique challenges face virtual, or dispersed, teams and we offered tips to help with efficient new product development using this type of team.

Key Learning Points

Let's review the key points addressed in this resource.

Innovation is important to the long-term success of any business. We can categorize new product development projects into several types, depending upon the market and technical risk of the innovation effort. We also learned that cross-functional NPD teams can be structured to best match the project type. For example, a breakthrough project involves higher risk with potentially higher reward and should be worked by a venture team. Projects with lesser complexity, such as platform projects and some derivative and enhancement projects, can be worked by a full team. Less complicated derivative or enhancement projects are addressed by lean teams while incremental improvement projects can be executed by a functional work group.

Effective new product development also requires a strong leader who can clearly define the common goals and purpose of the project. Additionally, the leader is responsible to provide an open organizational culture that can enhance the innovation experience to deliver new products in an effective and efficient manner. Virtual teams present special considerations and we've offered several tips and techniques to enhance the effectiveness of these dispersed teams.

How Much Do You Remember?

Test your knowledge by answering the following questions.

Imagine that your firm markets a line of organic, whole-grain muffins baked in a wood-fired oven. Mark (**X**) in the box preceding your response.

1. Your customers request donuts as an additional breakfast food. What type of NPD project is this?

☐ a. Product Improvement

☐ b. Line Extension

☐ c. Derivative

☐ d. Breakthrough

2. What type of innovation team should your firm use to develop and market the new donut line?

☐ a. Functional work group

☐ b. Lean Team

☐ c. Full Team

☐ d. Venture Team

3. Your customers have also requested banana bread as an additional breakfast item. This project type is

☐ a. Product Improvement

☐ b. Line Extension

☐ c. Derivative

☐ d. Breakthrough

4. What type of innovation team would you use to develop the banana bread product?

☐ a. Functional work group

☐ b. Lean Team

☐ c. Full Team

☐ d. Venture Team

5. Suppose one of your muffin distributors suggests selling your muffins to a large supermarket chain. This type of project is

☐ a. Product Improvement

☐ b. Line Extension

☐ c. Derivative

☐ d. Breakthrough

6. The type of NPD team that would be best suited to adding the new distribution channel for your organic muffins is

☐ a. Functional work group

☐ b. Lean Team

☐ c. Full Team

☐ d. Venture Team

7. Your chef accidentally discovers that adding lemon peel to the muffin recipes significantly enhances the flavor is enhanced significantly, and a panel of taste testers agrees that the lemon peel does not change the texture or quality of the muffin in any other way. This type of project is

☐ a. Product Improvement

☐ b. Line Extension

☐ c. Derivative

☐ d. Breakthrough

8. Which type of team would you use to commercialize the lemon flavor enhancement in the muffins?

☐ a. Functional work group

☐ b. Lean Team

☐ c. Full Team

☐ d. Venture Team

Check Appendix 1 for the correct answers.

Next Steps

This is your opportunity to consider what you have learned and how you can best apply these new strategies.

As you begin to manage innovation projects, you should carefully consider the degree of technical and market risk. Often those projects with the higher levels of risk also have a higher potential for reward. However, more complex innovation projects should be coupled with a cross-functional team that can deliver the new product effectively.

If you are currently managing an innovation program, be sure to check Table 2 and align your project team structure with the recommended type to match the complexity and risk of the innovation effort. Careful attention to team structure, organizational culture, and leadership can lead to long-term success in innovation.

Appendix 1

References and Answers

Wheelwright, Steven C and Kim B. Clark. *Revolutionizing Product Development: Quantum Leaps in Speed, Efficiency, and Quality.* New York: The Free Press, 1992.

Glossary

- Breakthrough = an innovation project that develops a new product using new technologies and is sold commercially into a new market.

- Cross-Functional Team = a team of innovation workers who represent each function necessary to complete the work and are empowered to represent the project in their home organization(s).

- Derivative = a type of innovation project that involves adding features or other new technologies to an existing product that is sold in current markets, and is often deployed as part of a platform project over time.

- Extension = sometimes called a line extension, this type of project will have minor technology improvements to sell a product into new markets.

- Functional work group = this type of team works primarily on low risk, low uncertainty new product development projects with little interaction across functions or departments.

- Full team = an innovation team that works cross-functionally to develop a complex innovation with a high degree of technical uncertainty for new or emerging markets.

- Improvement = a type of new product development project that involves little technology development for a product that is sold primarily into existing markets; an example is the cost reduction project.

- Incremental innovation = a small improvement in the technology of a product that is already sold into an existing commercial market.

- Innovation = the process of commercializing a new or improved technology into an existing or new market.

- Lean Team = a cross-functional team that involves part-time team members and a part-time team leader. The team is used to develop new products with low technical risk and/or few market development requirements.

- NPD = new product development.

- Permanent team = an organizational structure composed of a group of people that work on routine day-to-day tasks for as long as the organization exists.

- Platform = a special type of breakthrough project in which a new product is developed with a common architecture that will be utilized long-term for a variety of new products.

- R&D = research and development.

- Radical innovation = technology that is brand new in the marketplace.

- Team = a small group of people with complementary skills who are committed to a common purpose and who hold themselves mutually accountable.

- Temporary team = a group of workers who are assembled for a short time to accomplish a specific task or set of tasks.

- Venture team = a highly coordinated, co-located team that is used to develop new to the world technologies and markets.

- Virtual Team = a group of workers who are dispersed geographically and communicate primarily via asynchronous and electronic means.

Test Your Knowledge Answers

Chapter 1
Why is New Product Development (NPD) Different?

The bookkeeping staff at your firm prepares the monthly financial reports and assists with special requests for data. Would you consider this team a permanent or temporary team? Why?

Answer: The bookkeeping staff is a permanent team to conduct day-to-day work. Specific individuals may come and go as job assignments change, but the team structure is maintained over the long-term.

Chapter 2
Types of NPD Projects

Suppose your firm manufactures pencils. A member of your sales team comes to you and indicates that he has learned of a large demand for colored pencils that have red points on one end and green points on the other end. What type of NPD project is this and why?

Answer: The double-ended color pencil is a breakthrough project since the commercial market has high uncertainty and will require substantial development. Additionally, your firm does not have the technical experience yet to install two different colored "leads" into a single pencil.

Chapter 2

Your company manufactures pet food. One very popular product line is tuna for cats. You currently sell tuna in cans and are considering selling a tuna/salmon blend as well. You are also considering selling a tuna/whitefish blend in cans and a flaked tuna product available in snack-sized portions. Describe these innovation projects.

Answer: Tuna is a platform product for the pet food company. The tuna/salmon and tuna/whitefish blends are considered derivative products. The snack-sized tuna portion may be either a derivative product or a line extension product, depending upon the market penetration that the firm has with typical the pet food customers and the expertise of the company to package snack-sized portions.

Chapter 3

Suppose you have a team composed of Larry, an electrical engineer; Mary Kay, an electronics specialist; and Lee, a journeyman electrician. The team is tasked with adding a circuit breaker to the factory. Is this a cross-functional team?

Answer: No, the team members all represent the same function and likely report to the same department manager. They are working on a simple project without a strong element of innovation.

Chapter 3

Is it possible to use a full team for a new product development project that is also a new platform?

Answer. As you learned in Chapter 4, radical innovations are best executed by a venture team. However, depending upon the complexity of the technical innovation and the market requirements, it is possible to utilize a full team with proper organizational constraints for a platform development project.

Chapter 4
Matching Innovation Project and Team Type

Suppose the company already has extensive expertise in solar-powered engines and markets the solar-powered engines on children's toys, like wagons and radio-controlled cars. What type of project and what type of innovation team would you recommend now?

Answer: Because the company has extensive expertise with solar-powered engines, the technical innovation is not as risky, so the project may be a line extension into the new market of bicycles. There is some uncertainty in the market development, so a full team is likely the best type of team to execute this project. If the firm has already penetrated the bicycle market, a lean team may even suffice due to the lower risk.

How Much Do You Remember Answers

Answers:

1. d. Breakthrough
2. d. Venture Team
3. c. Derivative
4. b. Lean Team
5. b. Line Extension
6. c. Full Team
7. a. Product Improvement
8. a. Functional work group

Appendix 2

About . . .

About This Book

Goals and Objectives

Our goal is to provide education-based and competency-based learner resources that are easy to use, relevant to today's fast-paced and complex business environment, written by thought leaders in their fields, competitively priced, and accessible online for printing and distributing locally.

Adult Learners

All of our resource materials are designed and developed for adult learners and the learning strategies that work best with them. Adult learners expect—and deserve—to conclude the experience with competencies that can be applied directly and immediately on the job. Participants must be able to recognize and use the competencies in real job situations or "training-in-context."

A blend of content presentation, group exercises, open dialogue, and opportunities for interaction rank high among the most useful learning techniques for emphasizing a "training-in-context" concept, in which the learning environment approximates the workplace environment in as many contextual ways as possible. This is characteristic at all levels within the organization. And, by using this approach, participants will be confident in the use of their newly acquired skills and competencies on the job.

Those who participate in and complete this course should be able to demonstrate their understanding of the concepts and principles contained in the text and/or presented in the instruction.

About the Author

Teresa Jurgens-Kowal, Ph.D.

Teresa is president of Global NP Solutions, LLC, and a strategic innovation provider. She is an accomplished visionary and results-oriented professional with extensive industry experience from creative research to effective portfolio management through streamlined new product development processes.

Prior to founding Global NP Solutions, Dr. Jurgens-Kowal acquired over 12 years experience in leadership and management positions with ExxonMobil Chemical Company and 17+ years as a practicing chemical engineer. Her corporate career encompassed various functions, including New Product Development, Portfolio Management, Licensing, Marketing, Logistics and Supply Chain, Manufacturing, Project Management, and Research Technology.

Teresa has extensive experience leading successful teams, managing the product development life cycle, and defining the portfolio strategy. Her deep expertise in intellectual property management, product and process licensing, portfolio planning, customer service, and various business processes make her an ideal teacher and trusted advisor who knows both the theory and practices of New Product Development.

About the Ryan Group of Companies

What We Offer

We offer high-impact, high-value situational learning products and services in the form of online, web-accessible resources.

Our business units and brands

The Ryan Group, Inc.

Get to the Point Books

Learning and Development Center

Case-Based Curriculum

Business Simulations

We design, develop, and deploy total packaged solutions that focus on the integration of learning, knowledge, and assessment to drive performance and business results. www.ryangroupinc.com

Get to the Point Books

Online digital training resources (retail web-store).
www.gettothepointbooks.com

Learning and Development Center

LMS platform and digital content library with integrated competency assessment and modeling.
www.learninganddevelopmentcenter.com

Business Simulations

Business simulations for change, strategy, cost mapping, and creativity and innovation. www.tabletopsimulations.com

www.ingramcontent.com/pod-product-compliance
Lightning Source LLC
Chambersburg PA
CBHW080937040426
42443CB00015B/3451